THUMBSUCKER

by the same author

Can't Not Won't
A Story About a Child Who Couldn't Go to School
Eliza Fricker
ISBN 978 1 83997 520 2
eISBN 978 1 83997 521 9

The Family Experience of PDA
An Illustrated Guide to Pathological Demand Avoidance
Eliza Fricker
Foreword by Ruth Fidler
ISBN 978 1 78775 677 9
eISBN 978 1 78775 678 6

of related interest

The Educator's Experience of Pathological Demand Avoidance
An Illustrated Guide to Pathological
Demand Avoidance and Learning
Laura Kerbey
Illustrated by Eliza Fricker
ISBN 978 1 83997 696 4
eISBN 978 1 83997 698 8

Nurturing Your Autistic Young Person
A Parent's Handbook to Supporting Newly
Diagnosed Teens and Pre-Teens
Cathy Wassell
Illustrated by Eliza Fricker
Foreword by Emily Burke
ISBN 978 1 83997 111 2
eISBN 978 1 83997 112 9

Thumb-sucker

Written and illustrated by
Eliza Fricker

The Stories of Our Lives: Therapeutic
Reflections by Naomi Fisher

Jessica Kingsley Publishers
London and Philadelphia

First published in Great Britain in 2024 by Jessica Kingsley Publishers
An imprint of John Murray Press

1

Copyright © Eliza Fricker 2024

The right of Eliza Fricker to be identified as the Author of the Work has
been asserted by her in accordance with the Copyright, Designs and
Patents Act 1988.

The Stories of Our Lives: Therapeutic Reflections
Copyright © Naomi Fisher 2024

Front cover image source: Eliza Fricker.

A CIP catalogue record for this title is available from the British Library
and the Library of Congress

ISBN 978 1 83997 854 8
eISBN 978 1 83997 855 5

Printed and bound in Great Britain by TJ Books Limited

Jessica Kingsley Publishers' policy is to use papers that are natural,
renewable and recyclable products and made from wood grown in
sustainable forests. The logging and manufacturing processes are expected
to conform to the environmental regulations of the country of origin.

Jessica Kingsley Publishers
Carmelite House
50 Victoria Embankment
London EC4Y 0DZ

www.jkp.com

John Murray Press
Part of Hodder & Stoughton Ltd
An Hachette Company

Acknowledgements

To Jess, Laura, Charlie and Alice for making this less scary and being there for all those chats always. I could not have done any of this without you lot.

To Katy and Anya for all the times you have listened and stayed and never judging, even when you might think it's not such a good idea.

To all my friendships old and new, you mean more than I always show.

To Vauna for helping me say those things I've been too scared to say out loud.

And B, you are my driving force, always. x

Introduction

This book tells the story of growing up different. It takes ownership of the names I was called. I know now that those names weren't nice and only taught me to hide my difficulties more. I grew up feeling ashamed and questioning who I was.

It was exhausting.

It was confusing.

I hid myself.

I wasn't doing it on purpose. I was actually finding lots of things really hard and exhausting. Those names didn't help, they just made me feel bad (a lot of the time). But I feel passionate about not just accepting this. And not accepting some of the roles that pigeon-hole and define the female experience in particular. Now I want to say – just because that's how it was then doesn't mean it was okay.

We can say this together. It might be hard to acknowledge, but the sky won't fall down. We can rewrite our own narratives, forgive those who didn't know or understand, and teach those who are in a position to do better to try harder. To listen.

Thumbsucker.
How it all began...

Lamb, my thumbsucking aid since I was born.

Lamb didn't resemble one for very long.
He soon became very worn...

And was often mistaken as trash.

And I was always being hassled to stop.

I never wanted to give up.

Even as I got older...

But I didn't like the attention it drew.

And when I got my first boyfriend he made it quite clear how he felt about it.

And one day after a big row, desperate for comfort, I really needed him.

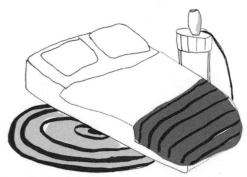

But Lamb had gone, along with the boyfriend. I never found him again.

DOGS FOOD TOILETS SMELLY FRIENDS

Worrying was so embedded in my day to day life, there was even a running joke in my family that I would worry if I didn't have anything to worry about.
Worry was a constant in my life, it felt like every day there was something.
It was a weight I carried, but I was also very aware of the impact this had on those around me.

Places we visited spontaneously were full of unknowns. For a period of time, I was most worried about dogs.

Dogs were loud and unpredictable. I didn't want to be anywhere near them, reassurance was not helpful - it actually made me feel worse.

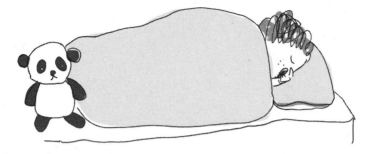

I napped all the time...

...and anywhere.

There were only a few foodstuffs that I would eat.
This caused some problems over time.

Family holidays could end with me having meltdowns because I would be hungry and not know what to eat.

Which would try even my normally patient parents and leave me feeling guilty for ruining special occasions.

Different foods gave me stomach aches and hurt my mouth ulcers...

Which made eating out tricky...

Or going to friends' houses.

Panic, anxiety and pressure to eat unknown foods could lead to a feeling my throat was closing up or tightening.

So I preferred food at home where my parents knew what foods I would eat as well as what could comfort me in equal measure.

School was worse...

Trying to talk to distract...

It has stayed with me, anyone I see drinking milk out of a carton still brings me the same revulsion.

HYPOCHONDRIAC

We had been practising a school dance for weeks...

I liked rehersals, but the thought of performing was starting to make me feel worried...

The pressure, the worry, about getting the dance right meant I didn't feel well enough on the day of the dance.

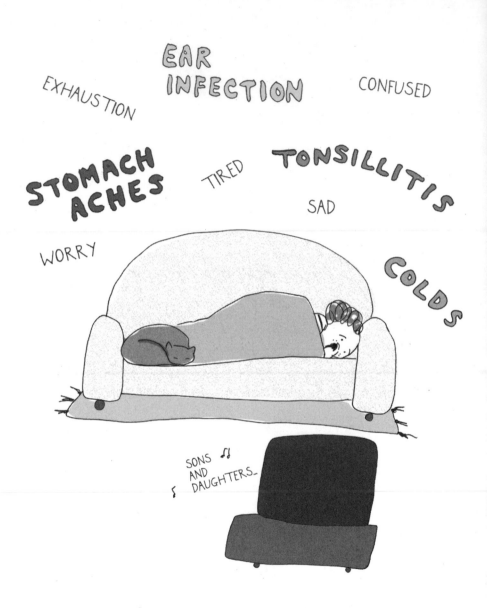

I had so many days off, and while I did seem to get ill a lot this would often be a combination of emotional things too.
Staying at home was quiet, comfort, safety, consistency. I wanted to be there as much as I could.

Not being at home caused other problems.
School toilets began a lifelong issue...

The dirt, the smells, the freezing cold and
the lack of privacy. I learnt quickly not to go.

Causing stomach issues that have stayed with me.

FICKLE

There was an ice skating couple that seemed to be always on TV in the 1980s and I wanted to be just like them.

I knew I would have to give it my best sell, I had
already tried a few other hobbies and not pursued them...

So eventually my hard sell won me some ice skating lessons but I soon realised I didn't like the heavy uncomfortable boots...

And I wasn't going to be swirling and sliding around for a long time.

MORE **UNIFORMS**   MORE **RULES**   MORE **DEMANDS**

Girls' Brigade and Guides were just like school, rules and regulations, and all the mean, bossy girls from school went to them too, so I didn't want to go.
Even Woodcraft Folk was organised.
Worst of all they all required you to go away from your parents and my crippling homesickness put short shrift to that.

But mostly it would be an image of something I would like and think I would like to be...

And then the reality would be so starkly different and disappointing...

It was nothing like I imagined, the carry case was smelly and dirty, and after playing it a while my spit dribbled out the end. I hated it.

There was horse riding on the heath and my dad paid some older girls to take me out on their horses.

The horses were unpredictable, easily spooked and smelly. It was uncomfortable and the girls were intimidating.
Overall it was not fun at all and there was the added worry of all the dogs at the stables.

I wanted to like something and stick to it. I had friends with grade 8 piano and black belts in karate, but it seemed so hard to find out what I liked apart from drawing or TV.

It would be a pattern late into life of trying seemingly random options and often ditching them for something else. I didn't seem to be able to make up my mind like other people... I needed to learn through doing.

SPOILT

My soft toy collection took up most of my bed. I loved them deeply, every one of them had a personality and I felt an enormous commitment to all of them...

I had a responsibility to all of them.

But it seemed most people didn't share my values...

Pretending I am fine in the hope she goes quickly...

Often I would feel a deep longing when I saw a soft toy.
There would be a strong sense of connection to it, I felt
I had to have it. Sometimes I sensed that it needed me too.
Monkey soft toys were always a sure bet... I would have
done anything to have owned one.

And I loved the ritual of looking at every new soft toy with my mum.

Mudlarking.

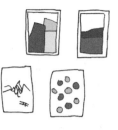

Postcards.

COLLECTIONS

I've always collected different things. Some have been brief obsessions, others have stayed long term...

Trainers.

These can be specific like my collection of flocked animals.

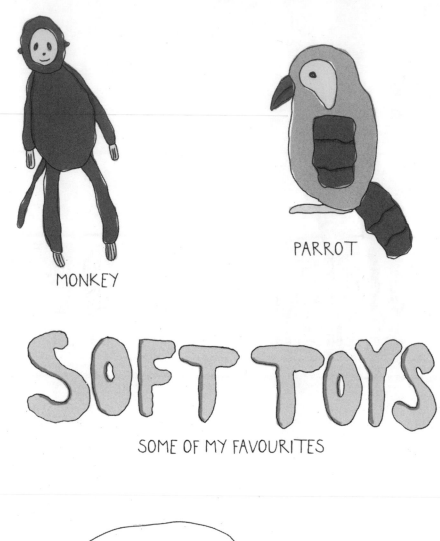

MONKEY

PARROT

SOFT TOYS

SOME OF MY FAVOURITES

DUCK

LAMB
(Ultimate number one)

Charity Shop Buys.

Scrapbooks.

Kinder Egg Toys.

Comics/Art Books.

Seashell Ornaments.

Snowdomes.

My collections are neatly organised. The balance of colours and textures give me a deep sensory joy. Along with the emotions and feelings I attach to them all...

Being surrounded by my stuff and knowing it all has a place is deeply comforting and reassures me. My things are safe and constant.

CONTRARY

Early experiences of clothes, socks and shoes could be tricky and contradictory...

I loved the measuring for shoes...

DEEP JOY

The pressure and sensation of having my feet measured was deeply satisfying.

What do you think?

Not sure...

Nice?

The smell of fresh shoes
was wonderful.
But the pressure to decide...

...would soon turn to rage as the agony
of the new shoes set in...

I always felt conflicted with clothes.
I wanted to look nice...

But the reality was they
felt uncomfortable and
made me feel weird and cross.

So I learnt what I loved and then clothing
brought me happiness and contentment.

My Favourite Sweatshirts of all Time.

The hot air balloon was padded vinyl and squeaked when it was pushed.

I had a special interest in the Pink Panther, so this ticked all the boxes.

My reversible Winnie the Pooh sweatshirt.

It was puffy and soft.

And then I discovered navy blue sweatshirts. Swoon.

But my all time favourite is still a grey sweatshirt. The marl tone of the grey, the right neckline... Still soothes me.

Ginger, curly and full of Knots...

I wanted those French plaits, swinging silky pony tails and sleak fringes of the popular girls.

But the tight curls, frizz and reluctance to brush it was always frustrating, painful and disappointing.

I knew I would never fit in and be like those groups of girls who laughed and chatted with shiny hair.

PAIN

While my imagination often brought comfort
it also caused frustration...

I would find it so hard to change track once I felt or believed something.

And while I probably seemed fussy it was just that it was so hard for me to think or see things differently once it was in my head.

These episodes would leave me exhausted and often end with me going for long, deep sleeps.

I just seemed to think about things so differently to other people, so I learnt to hide a lot of it away...

I learnt how much my emotions impacted others as I got older, so I started to conceal them more and more.

HOMESICKNESS

Bastille Festival
Year 7 Residential

School trips were the worst, as I couldn't escape.

1991 Turkey.
Unicorn Theatre Trip.

The environment was so different to what I was used to. My chaperone phoned my dad, but hearing his voice just made me more upset...

Homesickness isn't just about the food, it's the sense of the place, even the aesthetics.
It's a feeling of being uprooted, of not belonging, worry and a lack of security when there is little of what you know and the things you need to feel safe.

DIFFICULT

I didn't want to ruin days out or spoil holidays.
I didn't want those meltdowns to be remembered more
than the sun or the beach or the time we had a villa
and a pool.
I wanted to have a good time.
But I knew I was the one who spoilt stuff, who made
others sad, angry and upset.
I confused people and I disappointed them.
Why couldn't I just eat the sandwich?
It was cheese and bread just like I have at home but
it wasn't.
It tasted different and I was already tired, sunburnt,
confused and anxious.
I didn't do it on purpose, it wasn't because I didn't want
to have a nice time.
I didn't want to upset you.
It wasn't just the cheese sandwich.
It was all too much.

HATSWORTH JUNIOR SCHOOL

NAME Eliza Fricker CLASS Amber

ENGLISH	good, could talk less
HISTORY	Very good + interested Lots of chatty!
GEOGRAPHY	Good. Too much chatty
ART	Excellent!
PE	More PE, less chatty
MATHS	Very talkative

'Bright' and 'able', but most reports and parents evenings would say I talked in class too much…

I was a constant doodler along with chatting. I couldn't concentrate without scribbling in the back of my exercise books. It calmed and soothed me. This is a page from one of my secondary school work books.

I was always chatting with classmates but it was so confusing. I tried so hard, and to outsiders it would probably appear that I had lots of friends, but I often had fallings out, got too involved or was left on the outskirts. I found it all exhausting.

Shall we pretend they are all going to a party?

So I preferred one really close friendship where we played out imaginary lives with our dolls and this was deeply fulfilling and much more fun.

To avoid the confusion of playtimes I would often spend time with the dinner ladies whose normal chatter would remind me of my mum and nan and give me comfort and reassurance.

I would often become obsessed with certain teachers...

At home that evening...

The walk to school was long but I loved it...

My dad and I had our own games including The Worst Garden Awards...

And a whole array of characters we looked out for...

Those walks to and from school seemed to go on and on, they were a time of just free flow talking that could go any which way and I loved them.
I still think it's where I felt truly relaxed and happy, just walking and talking without fear of judgement.

The next morning on my way to school I am bursting to tell anyone I can the amazing story...

I felt the shame and embarrassment hard and still do.
I feel it easily and try to avoid the humiliation I associate
with it even today.

FREAK

As I got older I seemed to meet more people who would seek me out even when I tried to avoid them...

I didn't understand why this happened...

Because sometimes they would act like they wanted to be friends...

I'd saved for months for that Game Boy. My dad had even given me a vintage camera case to protect it. I thought I looked cool but it probably just made me stand out even more.

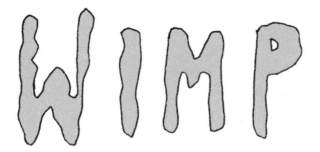

WIMP

I was so distraught watching The Neverending Story that my dad had to rewind the video of the horse dying.

And the organist's monkey dying in another film I watched left me sobbing for hours.

I don't think I could listen to the theme music from The Littlest Hobo ever again.

So many things were just too risky, and so as I got older I learnt to cover my fears with bravado and witty cynicism.

This also meant while I had a lot of friends, I also stayed on the periphery as I missed out on stuff.

Often when things were too much for me.

Misunderstandings were commonplace in school...

*Actually swore (it was the 1980s) but omitted this.

Later that evening at home...

What made the whole thing worse was having to spend the whole day in my headteacher's hot, Rococo style office while my dad tried to sort it out.

I just wanted the whole thing forgotten...

Instead it wasn't, and it only taught me
not to speak out or make a fuss.

Role play helped me enormously when it came to processing my school days. I would replay everything by myself, taking control of situations.

For a long time I have had an imaginary set of cards in my head. Most are family members who made those early impressions or blueprints of different personality types.

When I meet someone new I think of that 'deck of cards'.

I would then know who I had to be with the deck of cards of people not really ever changing from its core set.

Which is also why groups of people were so much harder to manage. They made my technique tricky, because I would need to use more than one card.

Role play was such a comfort to me.
One of my favourite times was 'Post Office' where I would use all the stationery I collected to imagine I was in charge of stamping, mailing and form filling.

Another favourite was 'Tea Rooms'...

My parents owned a Victorian glass fronted
dresser that they filled with ceramics they collected...

I would climb on the kitchen chair and take them all out...

I felt a deep joy imagining a tea room
full of cakes and crockery.

Tea rooms would stay as my comforting thought.
When I felt overwhelmed, I would think about those
beautiful cakes. I think about them still.

Diagnosis Letter

Extracts from my diagnosis letter

Dear Eliza,

...You shared with me your insight, openness and creativity. I was delighted to hear about your passion for writing and drawing...

...Thank you for providing me with such in-depth and nuanced information about yourself now and in the past. On Zoom we explored your life experiences and individual traits, which helped me to understand you and your perspective on the world...

...You have clearly worked exceptionally hard to reach where you have in your life, while dealing with additional challenges that other people do not have to deal with. You have created a life that you can thrive in, working to your strengths in creativity and surrounding yourself with understanding and kind people. I hope with this improved self-understanding you will continue to thrive in life.

The Stories of Our Lives

THERAPEUTIC REFLECTIONS

by Naomi Fisher

Dr Naomi Fisher is a clinical psychologist who specialises in trauma, autism and alternative approaches to education. She is the author of two books, Changing Our Minds *and* A Different Way to Learn. *Her passion is helping people make sense of their experiences and differences in a way which does not blame or pathologize.*

One of the things which interest me most as a psychologist are the stories that humans tell. Some of these are formalised, written in books. We tell stories to our children when they are young. We tell them tales of imaginary lands, or stories about talking pigs and flying horses. We snuggle up for stories at bedtime and we choose carefully, we don't want to scare them or expose them to ideas that they aren't ready for.

Then there are the other, less formal, stories. The things which happen to us, and the way that we make sense of the world around us. Humans are driven to try and understand what is going on, right from early on when young children ask us 'Why?' several hundred times a day for what can seem like for ever.

How do we answer the 'why?' question? One of the ways is through the stories or narratives that we tell. The stories provide an explanation. 'This happened, because of this' or 'This happened to you, because of this'. There's a sense of resolution, of closure. We can breathe easy now because we understand.

I'm a trauma therapist, and one of the things which I do in the therapy room is listen to stories. It's an immensely privileged position to be in. For I don't just listen, but I try to help people make a different sense of the things which have happened to them, to find a meaning which allows them to move on with their lives. With young children this is often explicit. I write a story about the things which have happened to them. I make a guess about the explanations that they have found for themselves, and I write a new story. A child to whom bad things have happened will often have made sense of those things by deciding that it must be their fault or that they deserved it. I write a story which includes the idea that bad things sometimes happen to children, and that isn't the fault of the child they happen to. I tell them about the things which happened to them and which they didn't understand at the time, because they were too young. A child who was in a car accident before they were old enough to understand what was going on can grow up with an ongoing feeling that they aren't safe, but they don't know why they feel like that. Their memories are often fragmented and confused. Through stories, I make sense of their feelings and explain what happened. I give them a new narrative.

With adults, it's not always so clear that we are telling stories. Adults will come and tell me about the things they learnt about themselves growing up, and how those things still affect them now. We'll find the stories from when it began – that time when they had to stand in front of the class because they were talking, and how they thought 'This is because I'm bad'. The time when they didn't understand why the teacher didn't care about keeping to the rules as much as they did, and they thought 'There's something wrong with me'. The time when their parents were shouting and they were scared and felt powerless.

I work with adults to help them find new stories which enable them to move forwards in their lives. We go back and make sense of the things which happened to them from a different perspective. They find new meanings – maybe they weren't bad, but just young. They were powerless then, but not now. We can update the narratives, and in doing so, people are liberated from the old stories which kept them tied down.

Growing up female

The stories we learn to tell about ourselves are profoundly affected by the culture and time that we are born into. Although Eliza's illustrations will resonate with all readers. It is worth reflecting on the fact that women and girls in particular are given a limited set of roles to play in life. Not long ago in this country, and still today in many countries around the world, these roles were clearly stated and enforced. Girls were not allowed to get an education or work in particular jobs, for no other reason than that they were female. Women were told that getting married and having children would be their fulfilment, and that jobs should be chosen because they were 'family-friendly'. Not too demanding or absorbing, that's what family-friendly can be code for. Nothing that you'll lose yourself in, or that requires you to stay up at night. So that there's enough time and energy left for the housework and childcare, of which women still do the majority.

This has changed, at least in Britain. For the generation of British women which I am a part of, and which Eliza is a part of, we weren't (mostly) told explicitly that being female meant that we had to be a certain way. We weren't explicitly told that being a girl came with particular expectations and limitations – in fact, we were often told that we could be anything. That we could do anything and that we just had to dream big and reach for the stars. It was up to us.

And maybe that is one reason why it was so hard for many of us to see the ways in which we were corralled. We weren't told that we could only become a teacher or a nurse, as some of our mothers were. We didn't face the 'marriage bar', expected to give up work or marriage, as some of our grandmothers did. The ways in which society showed us how we were expected to behave, what it meant to be a girl and the things we learnt about ourselves along the way were more subtle for our generation. The way in which we learnt to hide who we were, in order to be more acceptable, not to rock the boat. The way in which we learnt to put up with discomfort, so that others would be more comfortable. The scripts we learnt to use with others, to hide our social discomfort and awkwardness. The ways in which we learnt to feel bad about ourselves. The masks we learnt to put on, so that the world wouldn't see how we really felt.

The way that these narratives show up in women's lives today are many. The media tell stories about what women should be, and what their experience should be, and advertisers exploit the way in which our lives don't measure up by promising that if we just buy this scented candle or that low-fat snack bar, things will be different. The difference between the experience of most women and the way that women are portrayed in the media is huge. Many women feel this as a personal failing. I meet women who feel that they have failed as a mother, because they are not fulfilled by spending their days finger-painting and changing nappies. I meet others who feel that the absence of children – whether chosen or not – defines them as having missed out of one of the crucial parts of women's narratives, one of the things which (they are told by society) should have been in their story. I meet many women who tell me that they have spent their lives serving other people's needs, putting them first, and they aren't sure when it's ever going to be their turn. I meet women who say they find it almost impossible to say no, to put their needs first, because they are so concerned about upsetting or being rejected by other people.

Space to think

We're at a time of social change. An increasing number of women are looking back over their lives and asking what they learnt about themselves growing up. More, they are asking what they were told about themselves along the way. They are reflecting on how they were encouraged to fit themselves into boxes, not to be too chatty, too sensitive, too emotional, too *much*. To stop being how they were, in order to fit into being what the world was telling them that they should be.

It's often not until they approach their 40s that women have space to reflect on what they learnt about themselves growing up. Until then, life can feel like a treadmill, with the next thing always on the horizon. Nursery, primary school, secondary school and then whatever comes next. Jobs, partners, children, each one follows the one before. Psychologists sometimes call these 'developmental tasks' or 'life stages'. What is expected of each stage of the human life cycle. Even if you don't conform, you often find yourself defined against those who do, or worrying that perhaps you should be in case you are 'missing out'.

This is particularly the case for women, because of biology. Many women tell me that they felt that everything in the first third of their life had to happen on schedule, that there was no time to waste. They couldn't fall behind, or they might never catch up. They feel a pressure to get a job, a partner, 'settle down', because if they didn't, it could all be too late. When they do have children (if they do), most of the care of those children still often falls to them, and in the early years this can mean having no space or time at all. It's not until their children grow a bit older and more independent that they start to have time to think, and to ask themselves how they got here, and what it was all about.

This is the point where many women start to ask themselves about the narratives which they accepted without question. They ask who the protagonist was in their story, and who drove the narrative.

When they look back over their lives, many women tell me that the question 'What do I want to happen?' was rarely at the forefront of their minds. They tell me how important it was for them to be liked by others when they were growing up, and how many of their decisions were based on pleasing others rather than themselves. They tell me about the weight of obligation which guides their decision-making, how they make choices so that others won't be inconvenienced. They tell me how intensely they feel it when someone doesn't like them, how rejected they feel and how it seems to reflect on their worth as a person. They tell me how they have cut the corners off themselves, in order to be more acceptable to others. In order not to upset them.

As women think back over their lives, and as they watch their children grow in their own lives, many of them start to rediscover the parts of them which got lost along the way. They realise that as they were growing up they had to squash parts of themselves, that they were pushed to conform to a mould which didn't fit. And when it didn't fit, they felt that the problem was them, not the mould or the pressure. They felt blamed for their lack of what they saw as conventionality. Blamed for their difference to everyone else. And they absorbed this into themselves. Their story became that they were not good enough, that there was something wrong with them.

For many women, this re-evaluation of their life comes with a diagnosis or self-identification in adulthood of autism or ADHD. It's often their children who are diagnosed first, and then they start to wonder about themselves. They see that they share many of the characteristics of their child, but that their differences were seen through a different lens during their childhood, one which made them feel blamed and shamed. They see that they felt that their differences were because they weren't trying hard enough, or were not good enough.

The diagnosis provides a new story. It can allow them to accept that their differences are just part of who they are. The diagnosis gives them a different way to think about themselves, and that can feel liberatory. It provides a way out of the blame. Many women feel that a diagnosis allows them to say, for the first time, *This is who I am* rather than *I shouldn't be like this*.

Whether a person should need a diagnosis to be able to say this is a good question (and I would like it if our society didn't require a diagnosis for acceptance of difference) – but the fact remains that, in our current time and place, many women *do* feel that this is what the diagnosis gives them. They feel that it gives a shape and a name to their differences, and it allows them to own themselves and their individuality, often for the first time. They feel that it allows them to stop blaming themselves for the ways in which they feel that they don't measure up to what society expects of women. It allows them to rewrite their story, with themselves at the centre.

Humans look for explanations in order to help us make sense. We want to know why something is happening. With children in particular, the reasons aren't always easy to find. They don't always know why they are behaving the way that they do, and they sometimes can't tell adults even if they do know. So instead, we give the children labels which say that the problem is them.

This is something which many autistic adults tell me. They say that they grew up feeling a sense of wrongness, of not being good enough. They tell me that they felt that their reactions were wrong, that they were seen as either too reactive or not reactive enough. When they got upset, it wasn't understood by the adults around them as upset, so they were blamed or punished. And they didn't know why it was so hard for them. It just was, and so they thought the problem was them. Again and again they tell me, *It wasn't safe to just be me.*

Rewriting the story

In this book, Eliza is rewriting her story. She tells us about her life, from the perspective of the child she was. She shows us the labels she was given as a child – or perhaps those that she found for herself, and she shows us what it felt like to her. Each of those labels is a narrative, and often a shameful one. Ones that people avoid talking about, and which can still hold shame for them, years later.

All the women I know have these labels, and we continue to tell these stories about ourselves well into adulthood. My own are not entirely the same as Eliza's, although we share many, including *fussy, difficult* and *weirdo. Bossy* was one of mine, and *messy. Loud* was another, with a friend's mother telling me that I sounded like a fishwife when I shouted at a boy to go away when he was bothering me. I remember at age 12 deciding that from now on I would be quiet, because people seemed to like quiet girls more. I can still remember the feeling of pushing my lips together, saying to myself that I would only talk calmly. I wouldn't take up too much space. I wouldn't say anything which might stop people liking me.

One of the things many women learn growing up is that they should be different to how they really are, that they should mask their true feelings in order to be acceptable to others.

Stories from the inside

By illustrating these names, Eliza reclaims them. She tells us the stories from the child's perspective, and in doing so she gives us a window into a different narrative. She rejects the fear and shame and puts herself back at the centre of her own story.

Eliza's illustrations take us back to the girl that she was. She explains what she was unable to explain then. She wasn't spoilt, when she refused to wear new clothes. They felt scratchy and unpleasant because she was sensitive. She wasn't being a hypochondriac when she said she felt too ill to perform in the school play – she was literally overwhelmed by the expectations and demands.

As she looks back, Eliza can see her own behaviour through a different lens, one that is less blaming and more accepting. There was always a reason why, and those reasons were real.

Her illustrations require us to think about the way that we talk about and treat our children, particularly when their behaviour doesn't fit with what we expect or want. They challenge us to look beyond the behaviour and to ask ourselves what our children are learning from the way that we talk to them and about them. For there are still children being told that they are fussy or difficult, and that this is their fault. So much of children's behaviour is still seen as 'wilful' – meaning intentional – when in fact it is a response to the way that they experience the world. We don't ask enough about the reasons why a child might be behaving the way that they do, and when we think we have found an explanation, we often stop asking altogether.

THUMBSUCKER

Sucking is one of the ways in which we are soothed as babies. The sucking reflex is there from birth, to enable babies to feed. When a baby finds their thumb, it can be the first time they can do something to help calm themselves. They put their thumb in their mouths, and they feel better. They relax.

This association between sucking your thumb and feeling soothed doesn't end after babyhood. Many children continue to suck their thumbs, but as they get older, adults try to dissuade them from it. 'You're too old now,' they say. You can even buy horrible tasting nail polish to put on children's thumbs, so that when they do put their thumb in their mouth the taste will stop them.

This means that thumbsucking can become a source of embarrassment and shame. This is odd, because when compared to many of the self-soothing strategies which adults use, such as drugs and alcohol, it is benign. There are few side-effects from thumbsucking and it's completely free.

The adult need to stop children sucking their thumbs seems to be connected to our fear that children won't grow up unless we push them out of each stage, that the job of adults is to make sure that children leave babyhood behind entirely. This doesn't just happen with thumbsucking. 'You're too old for this,' children are told, when they want to play, or to be picked up, or to sleep with their parents. We try to hurry them out of childhood, before they are ready. And so the children who need more soothing for longer are shamed.

WORRIER

When the world is a confusing place, it makes sense to worry. Children have little control over their lives, and when you know that meeting a dog, or a strong smell, will bring up intense feelings, worry can become a constant presence.

Adults often want children to be 'care free', but when the environment is unpredictable and possibly hostile, then sometimes worrying is all that children can do. They can't necessarily act upon their feelings, because they themselves don't have that power. They need to persuade adults to take their worries seriously, and this can make them worry even more, because they know that others don't want them to worry. Was there ever anyone who stopped worrying because they were told 'Don't worry'?

FUSSY

Eliza didn't like many foods growing up, and familiarity in food was really important to her. This was labelled 'fussy'.

Food is a flashpoint for many families. Having a child who 'eats everything' is a matter of pride for some parents, and so having a child who only eats a very restricted diet is the opposite. Many parents take it personally when their child doesn't eat the food they cook, and many adults feel able to comment on a child's food choices, either with approval (eats everything) or 'I would never have been allowed to get away with that' (has strong food preferences).

Eliza describes her throat closing up when she tried to eat unfamiliar food and the dread at the idea of food at a friend's house. I had my own food sensitivities as a child, and I remember the terrible feeling of being served a plate of ratatouille made of onions, courgettes and tomatoes (all my most hated foods) when visiting a friend. It wasn't just a dislike, it was as if my whole body rejected the meal. Each mouthful felt like torture, and had to be swallowed with a large glug of water.

HYPOCHONDRIAC

Hypochondriac means that you think that you're ill when you're not. It means you are too anxious about your health. It's never used in a positive way.

When a child has a physical reaction to the world around them, it is frequently dismissed. Schools tell parents to send their children with 'tummy aches' into school anyway, but tummy aches are one of the ways in which children show their distress.

It's very common for children to have physical symptoms when they are stressed – and in fact more common than we often acknowledge for adults too. Headaches, digestive problems, heartburn, all can be caused by stress, and yet we often say that stress-related symptoms are 'all in the mind' as if that means that they aren't real.

Physical symptoms in response to our environment are real. When I was unhappy at school as a child, my glands swelled up. When I was in a job which I disliked as an adult, my skin prickled every time I went in there. I developed headaches. These weren't because I was making it up, it was because my brain and body reacted to the environment in a very physical way.

FICKLE

Fickle means that you give things up too easily. You don't stick at anything and lack commitment.

This gap between what the child wants the world to be like and what it's really like can be vast. They'd like to be a competent musician or horse rider, but in fact the reality of being a beginner doesn't measure up to the dream, and it may be that they don't want to or aren't ready to put in the years of practice required.

When this happens and children want to quit, adults often won't let them. 'You need to learn to stick at things,' they say. And so they make children stick at things – or the children are shamed when they don't. The children are meant to learn the value of sticking with things, but sometimes they just learn that they won't be allowed to quit.

This can mean that children can't try out new things – at a time in their life which should surely be ideal for trying out new things without long-term consequences. For what does it really matter if they give up on the Brownies or the clarinet?

We rarely value giving children the opportunity to say no. We rarely celebrate their choices not to stick at something, to say that they aren't enjoying it. We see sticking at something as inherently superior, even if you're unhappy. It's a strange moral value which many of us carry into adulthood, finding it difficult to leave a job or relationship, even when it's clear that its time is up. We learn to doubt our instincts, to ask ourselves *Are you sure?*, just as we were asked in childhood.

SPOILT

Spoilt children. No one wants to be called spoilt, and no one wants to have a spoilt child. It's a word which blames both parents and children.

Being 'spoilt' is a judgement on children's behaviour. They are too entitled. They demand too much. They don't know their place. They expect their desires to be taken seriously, maybe they want to buy things and express how they feel when they can't do that. Maybe they have 'too many' toys.

But being 'spoilt' is also a judgement on parents, and a veiled warning to other parents. For 'spoilt' contains the idea that a child's behaviour is for a reason. It's because their parents have been too nice to them. They haven't enforced strict enough boundaries, they haven't said no enough – and so they've 'spoilt' their child. Like a cup of sour milk. No going back there.

Eliza liked collecting things as a child, particularly monkey soft toys, and if she saw one it was important to her to take it home. Eliza tells us here what all her soft toys meant to her, how each one felt like a personality to be cared for. Her possessions helped her feel safe, and her collections still do that for her today. But now she's an adult, and so no one calls her spoilt.

CONTRARY

Being contrary is an interesting story to tell, because it implies that a child is disagreeing, just for the sake of disagreeing. They are 'being contrary' when adults want them to do something, and they say no, or when they wanted something but then quickly realise that they have changed their minds. In Eliza's childhood, this was about clothes. She wants them, and then she can't wear them. She loves some aspects of getting new shoes, but actually wearing the shoes is painful.

When we don't understand why a child is behaving the way they do, it's easy to locate the problem in them and to become frustrated. 'Why can't they just behave?' we ask ourselves.

But it can be just as frustrating and confusing for them. They want something to be different, they want to love their new shoes or new clothes – but the reality is that they feel itchy and uncomfortable. Many children have sensory sensitivities, and these can render clothes intolerable. They don't understand why, but they learn quickly that only some clothes feel safe, and so they decide to stick to those.

They have found a solution which works – but then often that is a problem too. People tell them that they shouldn't be wearing the same clothes every day, or buying five of the same type of shirt once they find the right one. It's like they can't win. Either accept the agony of the uncomfortable clothes, or be mocked for wearing the same clothes every day. Otherwise, they risk being 'contrary'.

PAIN

Eliza was 'a pain' when what was in her head didn't match the world around her, and she couldn't make the shift. To the adults around her, it must have seemed like she was refusing to hear reality, but to her, it was just impossible.

The images in her head were so strong that she couldn't replace them with new ones, particularly when the new ones were less exciting and engaging. Who wants blobs of margarine instead of crisp butter curls, or a hairy man rather than a gorilla? She wasn't able to be flexible, and that wasn't a choice.

Being flexible and changing mental direction is something which children develop over time, and some find it much harder than others. It's a skill, but not one which is often acknowledged. She didn't want to be 'a pain', but she just couldn't take on new information fast enough for the world.

HOMESICKNESS

Finding it hard to be away from home is often called homesickness.

Homesickness implies that being away from home causes illness, but often it's more that being away from home means the loss of the things which enable a child to stay safe and calm. Strange food, strange people, no way to get away – children on residential trips have far less control over their environment than adults when they travel. Adults can choose to go and eat familiar food if they want to, or spend time in places which feel familiar.

Children are fully immersed in a way which rarely happens to adults, expected to stay with host families who may not speak their language, join in their life and eat their food. For some this is fine, for others it is profoundly anxiety-provoking and makes them very unhappy. They have little power to do anything about it. They can't choose to go home, even if they really want to.

DIFFICULT

Difficult is about how we are for other people. It's about their experience of us, as not conforming to what they would like us to be doing.

Difficult children are often those for whom things don't feel right, those who just can't find the right food to eat or settle down in a strange environment. They are the ones whose nervous systems are finely tuned, who struggle to keep themselves in balance. 'Difficult' babies won't be put down to sleep, they want to be carried around in the sling. 'Difficult' children don't conform easily with adult expectations and demands.

There are many reasons why girls and women are called difficult, and it can be because they refuse to keep quiet about how they are being treated. That difficult-ness is a strength, the part which says 'something isn't right here', and which agitates for change.

CHATTERBOX

Eliza's old school report tells us loud and clear – she was 'chatty', and this was a problem.

We talk about children's talking in a different way to adults. Specifically, children's talking can be too much and at the wrong times. A lot of school is about sitting and listening to the teacher, and children's conversations get in the way of that. We teach children that what the teacher wants to say is more important than what they want to say, and that they should be keeping quiet.

Talking and communicating is important way beyond what is actually said. When we talk to others, that's a way that we can connect, but also a way that we can regulate our emotions. Hearing comforting talk – like the dinner ladies – can be soothing, away from the rush and bustle of the playground. Eliza's doodles were another way that she regulated herself in class, and one which many children find, within the limited range of options they have available to themselves in the school environment.

Chatting or 'being chatty' is sometimes used to denigrate talk, particularly women's talk. When we say something is 'chat', we often mean that what is being said is not very important. It's 'just chatting' we say. But yet, as Eliza shows, 'just chatting' with her dad on the way to and from school was an essential part of connecting for her and helped her to manage her day. Talking doesn't have to be about what is actually said in order to be important.

GULLIBLE
Eliza believed what she was told – and others made fun of her for that.

Believing 'tall stories' will get you called gullible, but working out when people are being truthful and when they are joking is a skill which many find hard. Some find it difficult into adulthood. For many children it is impossible to tell whether a person is joking or not, leaving them in a world where nothing can ever quite be relied upon.

The other side of being gullible is being trusting. Gullible children trust the adults around them to be reliable and honest, and when this turns out not to be the case, the world feels like a less safe place. It can shatter their sense of safety and trust.

FREAK
It's easy to become a 'freak' growing up. Just having the wrong hair cut or clothes or wrong case for your Gameboy is enough, and then it makes you a target for bullies. At my school, having the wrong bag or socks was enough to make you a freak. The 'freak' implies that it's your fault they pick on you, because you're not like everyone else.

It takes many of us until adulthood to realise that, in fact, everyone else was faking it too. They were often consumed with anxiety that, one day, it would be noticed that their bag wasn't quite right. That the reason that people didn't speak up can be because they were terrified of the attention falling on them. Picking on someone who is different feels safe, because that way they protect themselves from becoming the 'freak'.

WIMP
Wimp means a weak and cowardly or unadventurous person.

Eliza felt things very intensely. She was sensitive to everything. She felt the deaths of animals on screen, so much so that she could not continue to watch. Her feelings of fear were so intense that she'd avoid taking risks, and she'd often retreat into sleep. Sleep was a safe place, somewhere where the overwhelm of all these emotions would subside for a while. The way this made sense for her at the time was that she must be a 'wimp', too weak to tolerate the things that others tolerated. She couldn't see that perhaps her feelings actually were more intense than other people's, perhaps the way that she experienced life simply was harder than many others.

WEIRDO
Misunderstanding social situations can quickly get you called a weirdo, particularly if you make any sort of fuss about it, and so many girls learn to hide what they are thinking or feeling in case they get it wrong.

Eliza's solution to being with others was to create an imaginary set of cards in her head, effectively prototype people. She'd fit the prototype to the person – were they more like her mum? Or her aunty? – and then she'd know how to behave. This worked fine as long as there wasn't more than one person in the group, because they might come from different cards and then she'd be stuck. How could she get it right for all of them?

DIAGNOSIS LETTER
Eliza's diagnosis letter offers a different narrative to the one of blame. It's a rejection of all the names which went before.

It is refreshingly positive. It talks about autism as a different neurotype – and thus provides a different lens through which to see her experiences.

Eliza's letter is neurodiversity-affirmative, and one of the ways in which it does this is by locating the cause of problems in non-autistic people and society, rather than (as often happens) in autistic people. It's a diagnosis which is a long way from the language of the diagnostic manuals it references, which are full of 'disorders' and 'impairments'. It rejects the medical model whilst also being part of it.

This letter tells another story about Eliza's life, one in which she has been working hard to manage in a world which wasn't designed for people like her, and crucially, that this wasn't and isn't her fault. This is a diagnosis which Eliza wanted, she asked for it and so it was under her control. For her, the diagnosis was an autonomous decision and was empowering. It felt like permission to be herself.

Afterword

Thumbsucking was a huge comfort to me, it calmed and soothed me. The toy lamb I carried with me made everything smell better too. My other comfort was always being with my parents – they understood me, they were lenient and allowed me to be. These were the two main things that made life a bit more manageable. Because lots of life was very hard.

Food was incredibly tricky, but I was fortunate as my parents were relaxed and accommodating with this. My diet consisted of mainly salad cream sandwiches, crisps and pancakes. They never grumbled about my lack of vegetables, they never complained when I didn't finish what was on my plate.

I was a collector from a young age and would follow current interests, such as parrots or monkeys. Mostly it would involve small things I could carry around to give me comfort and connection to home when I wasn't there, such as soft toys, small animals and erasers.

As I got older they changed into more 'acceptable' interests: fashion, music, comics, art. It was also a uniform that connected me to the right people. I held lots of attachment to all of these interests, whether it was my special fashion shop carrier bag collection to my small flocked animals. They provided comfort and consistency in an uncertain world.

I remained very uncomfortable and confused socially and preferred being at home and living with my parents but learnt to hide my sensory needs and anxieties with wit and cynicism, which got me out of situations without looking weak or difficult or weird with my peers. As long as I looked sarcastic and cool I thought I had pulled it off.

I was a top grade student at school but didn't do A-Levels, gap year travelling or university. Instead I stayed at home until I got married at 25. Now I realise this is the impact of making it through school and the toll it took. I also needed the comfort of close relationships, from my favourite teacher or dinner lady at school, to my parents and best friends I've kept for years and years, to intense romantic relationships. Comfort and connection. I have shared amazing times with these people and will never see this as a lack of independence, more a way to thrive through positive connection.

So diagnosis came late for me, partly because I had seemingly managed or coped through most of my life. I had hidden how hard so many things were for me, from filling out forms, to coping in different environments, such as doctors' surgeries. Speaking to official people left me situationally mute. But much of this appearing to be like everyone else had been at a cost to myself, my real self. I had hidden myself away, latching on to roles as a wife or mother to fit in.

And while most of this wasn't terrible, my sense of self was an abstract concept. I was whoever anyone wanted or expected me to be.

Growing up with the names I was called because people didn't understand me meant I learnt early on I was different. And I tried my whole life not to be, not to feel those feelings because no one else did.

So it wasn't until I started to work with the autistic community when I turned 40, finally doing work that felt meaningful and therefore fulfilling, that I started to grow in myself. These were people I felt instantly comfortable with, who saw me for me. I started to explore myself, have deeper conversations than I have ever had, and finally thought: perhaps I am autistic.

Diagnosis for me came fairly recently at 43, but with it some big life changes both liberating and scary. At times, I do feel extremely vulnerable, overwhelmed, and wonder if I will cope. However, I tell myself I am answerable only to myself – and finally it is my real self, not a constructed version for others to appear more likeable or easy.

Before diagnosis, this was my whole life, because when your early self is seen as not good enough or difficult, you hide it away and become what you perceive others would like you to be. But slowly I am learning to be me with the help of those who really see me for me, and this feels lighter, clearer, better than I have ever felt in my whole life. I am being honest and open, sharing what is hard, when I find things hard. I am not trying to be perfect any more.

And I am very proud to say I am still many things I have always been. I still collect things, I still have very specific sartorial choices, I still hate maths, but most importantly I am still the doodler and the chatterbox I was in school. Although actually, I have managed to make a pretty decent career out of it and this is what makes me happy.